DATE DUE			

SW   CO   MO
                 SP

COSTUME CRAFTS

By Iain MacLeod-Brudenell
Photographs by Zul Mukhida

Contents

Gareth Stevens Publishing
MILWAUKEE

6194369

About this book

Do you have one favorite thing you like to wear more than any other? Perhaps it's a printed T-shirt, a piece of jewelry, or a new pair of tennis shoes. This book is all about costume crafts. It shows how to make crafts from around the world and offers plenty of ideas to help you design your own.

In this book, you can find out about customs, crafts, and traditions based on different types of body decorations. At the back of the book, there is information on how to find out more about these crafts and traditions, with details about places to visit and books to read.

Some of the craft activities in this book are more complicated than others and will take longer to finish. It might be fun to ask some friends to help with these activities, such as making hats on page 4.

Before you start working on any of the craft projects, read through the instructions carefully. Most of the step-by-step instructions have a number. Look for the same number in the picture to see how to make each stage of your project.

Before you begin

Collect everything listed in the "You will need" box or general project directions.

Ask an adult's permission if you are going to use a sharp tool, dye cloth, or use an oven.

Prepare a clear work surface. If the activity is going to be messy, cover the surface with old newspaper or a waterproof sheet.

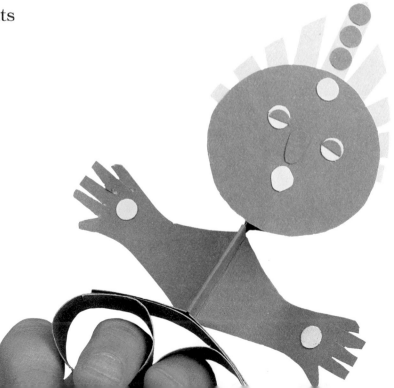

3

Hats

There are many reasons for wearing hats. When it is cold outside, a hat will keep you warm because you lose more heat from your head than from any other part of your body. People also wear hats to shade their heads from the sun, especially if they work outside. Firefighters and motorcyclists wear helmets for safety, while machine operators and nurses wear hats to keep their hair out of the way.

Hats are also worn for religious reasons. The Jewish kippah is a symbol of respect for God. And everyone is expected to cover their heads when going to a Sikh gurdwara, or temple. The men and boys wear a turban or a clean white cloth, and the women and girls wear a long scarf called a dupatta.

Hats can be fun, and they can make you feel special. They can also show that you are a member of a group.

Try making a hat

> **You will need:**
> - corrugated cardboard
> - scissors
> - white glue
> - transparent tape
> - a stapler
> - a balloon
> - a bowl
> - masking tape
> - newspaper torn into strips
> - a small bowl of wallpaper paste without fungicide
> - paint and materials for decoration

1 Cut a strip of cardboard about 2 inches (5 centimeters) wide that is long enough to go around your head. Put the band on your head and ask a friend to tape the ends together. Remove the band and fasten the joint securely with staples. Cut another strip of cardboard to fit over your head. Tape it in place at each side. Try on the frame. If it fits, remove it from your head and staple the strip to the band.

2 Blow up the balloon so that it just fits inside the cardboard frame. Tie a knot in the balloon. Rest it in a bowl to keep it still. You may need to use strips of masking tape to hold the frame in place on the bowl.

Dip strips of newspaper in the paste. Cover the frame with a layer of overlapping newspaper strips. Let it dry. Paste on another layer of newspaper and let it dry. Make about four layers of papier-mâché in this way.

When the papier-mâché is dry, remove the masking tape. Then lift the hat shape from the balloon. If it won't come off easily, pop the balloon.

1

2

Now paint and finish the hat in your own way. You can fasten a richly decorated front to make an Indian crown or add a cardboard brim and make lots of tissue-paper flowers for an Easter bonnet.

Silhouettes

A shadow can tell you some things about a person's appearance, but not everything. You can't be sure of the color of a person's skin, hair, or eyes from looking at a shadow, but you may be able to tell if he or she is a child, teenager, or adult.

If the shadow shows a side view of the person, you can see a profile. If it is someone you know well, you may be able to recognize his or her profile.

Silhouettes are portraits that are similar to shadows. A silhouette shows the outline of the head as a profile. Silhouettes are usually cut from black paper. Before photography was invented, silhouettes were very popular. People would pay a silhouettist to make portraits of family members and friends. In some European cities, there are still street artists who can cut a lifelike silhouette portrait in just a few minutes.

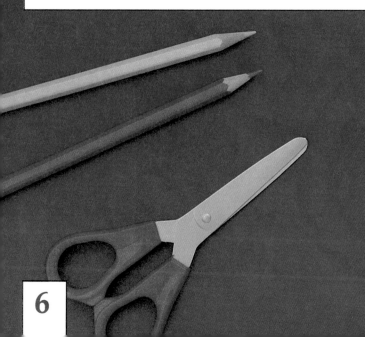

Try making a silhouette of a friend

You will need:
- a light
- colored or black paper
- thin, colored cardboard
- scissors
- a pencil
- white glue
- a paintbrush
- paint

Attach a large sheet of paper to the wall. Ask an adult to help you place a light about 10 feet (3 meters) away from the wall. Ask a friend to sit between the light and the wall. Switch on the light. There should be a clear shadow of your friend on the wall. Carefully draw around the outline of the head. You can either cut out the silhouette and glue it to a different colored piece of cardboard or fill in the outline with paint.

Try to make a paper frame or border for your silhouette.

6

7

Hairstyles

Some people wear their hair in a way that tells the world something about themselves or shows that they are a member of a group. For example, some Rastafarians wear dreadlocks as part of their religion, and Sikhs wear their hair long as one of the five duties of Sikhism.

People often choose a hairstyle they feel suits their personality and their way of life. Sometimes this means curling straight hair, straightening curly hair, or changing the color. Some swimmers even shave all their hair off as they try to make their bodies more streamlined.

In western Africa, hair plaiting is an art form. The braided patterns can take many hours to make.

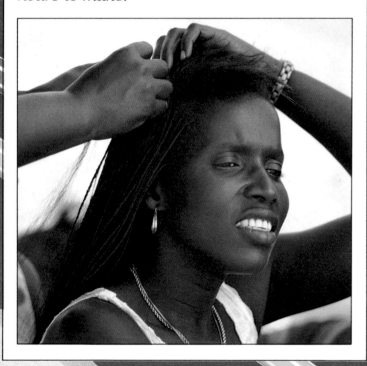

8

Try changing your hairstyle

You will need:
- a small photograph of your head and shoulders
- chinagraph pencils or spirit-based, felt-tip pens
- a piece of acetate (from an art shop)
- masking tape

Use masking tape to attach the photograph to the acetate. Draw a new hairstyle onto the acetate.

If you are using chinagraph pencils, you can wipe the acetate clean with a damp cloth and then try another style. Or, if you have a large enough piece of acetate, try moving the photograph along and drawing several more hairstyles to see which you like best. You can change the color of your hair, too.

You can also cut a new hairstyle from paper and put it on your photograph.

If you and a friend have photographs that are the same size, and if you are allowed to cut them up, you can change hairstyles. Cut around the faces and then swap hairstyles.

You can change your real hairstyle for fun, without cutting it, of course. **Ask permission first**. Try plaiting your hair or combing it a different way, or use hair gel that will wash out afterward. Does a different hairstyle make you feel any different?

Masks

Masks are worn for many reasons. Surgeons wear them to protect their patients from infection, and football players wear helmet-masks to protect them against injury.

The most common use for masks is in dance, drama, or to tell a religious story. A person's appearance is changed by a mask because it helps to hide his or her identity. So a mask can represent an animal, a god, or a character from a story. Sometimes masks are used to make people laugh or to frighten them.

Masks can be simple or decorated with feathers, paint, fur, and even jewels.

Try making a mask

You will need:	
• scrap paper	• paint
• thin cardboard	• a pencil
• scissors	• a paintbrush
• white glue	• elastic
	• a wooden stick

1 Fold a piece of scrap paper in half. Draw the outline of half a face, the same size or a little bigger than your own. Cut around the outline. Draw where you think the eyes and nose are. Cut along these lines. Try it on. If the eyes and nose are not in the right place, try again. Make the real mask from cardboard, using your practice mask as a guide.

2 Cut out a paper nose with tabs to fit the mask.

3 Try making a decorated mask.

To make the mask stay on your head, you can attach elastic at either side of the mask, glue the mask to a stick, or fasten the mask to the front of a simple cardboard frame (see page 5).

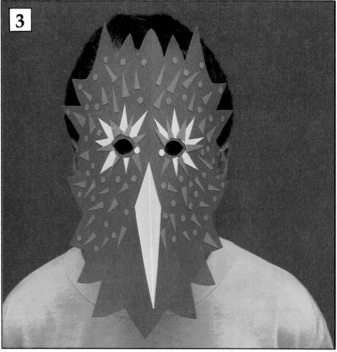

3

Try making a mask of a famous person. Find a large photograph of a celebrity in a magazine. Stick it onto cardboard and cut it out. Don't cut out the eyes, but ask an adult to help you use a craft knife to make a crescent-shaped cut beneath each eye of the picture. Push out the flaps of paper so you can see through the mask. Attach your mask to a stick. Now you can pretend to be a "star."

Transformation masks

Masks not only change the way people look; masks can also appear to "transform" people as they take on the character of the mask. The mask shown here does even more — it transforms itself to show different emotions. It is based on a clever idea of the Kwakiutl people of Canada. An actor wears a transformation mask of, perhaps, a wolf or the sun. At a dramatic point, he or she pulls a string, and the mask splits open to reveal another mask of a raven or a human face, such as the one pictured below.

Try making a transformation mask

You will need:
- plain paper
- white glue
- scissors
- paints or felt-tip markers
- a paintbrush
- scrap paper or material
- face paints
- a large box, one that is big enough to fit your head inside and has flaps that meet at the top

1 The top of the box, which has flaps opening out from side to side, will be the front of the mask. Cut a hole on one side of the box that is big enough for your head to fit through. The top of the box with the flaps should now be positioned to cover the front of your face, as pictured at the right.

Decorate the outside and inside of the flaps of the box with paints or make a collage from paper or pieces of scrap material.

2 When you wear this mask, try painting your own face with face paints or wearing a different mask underneath, such as the mask shown on page 11. When you wear your transformation mask, you can quickly change from one character to another by opening and closing the front flaps.

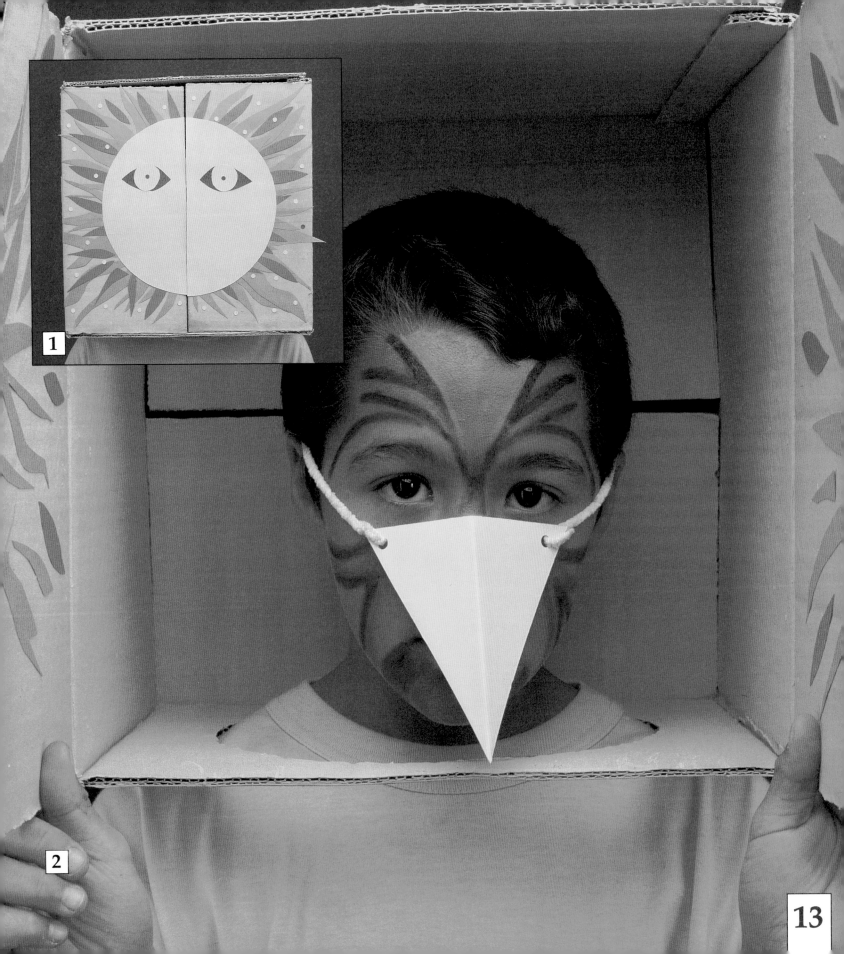

Necklaces

Necklaces are probably one of the oldest ways of decorating the body. They can be made of gold, precious jewels, beads — or of everyday materials like shells and paper.

The Zulu people of Africa weave strands of threaded beads together into intricate patterns. Often, many strands are knotted together to form a thick rope necklace.

Try making a necklace based on Zulu beadwork

For this necklace, the beads are not threaded, but poured into a plastic tube.

You will need:
- plastic tubing from an aquarium shop
- tiny beads
- glitter
- scraps of shiny paper or foil
- a button
- latex-based glue
- two large, round beads that just fit into the tube
- strong thread
- a large darning needle
- a small funnel that fits the tubing

1 Cut enough tubing to make a necklace that hangs loosely around your neck. Thread the needle. Tie one of the larger beads about 4 inches (10 cm) from one end of the thread. Hold the tube straight, drop the needle in, and pull the thread through. Put some glue on the sides of the bead and jam it into the end.

2 If you don't have a funnel, roll a piece of paper to make one. Pour some beads down the funnel into the tube and shake the tube to make the beads go right to the end. You can add the beads, glitter, and pieces of foil in any order, or you can make a pattern with them.

3 Tie a bead to the thread at the open end of the tube and glue it in place. Attach the button to one end of the thread. Make a loop at the other end that is big enough to go over the button. Tie it so it doesn't slide. To fasten the necklace, slip the button carefully through the loop.

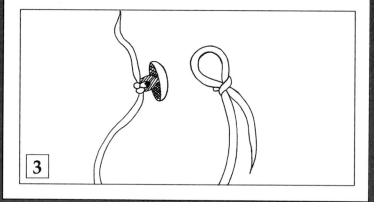

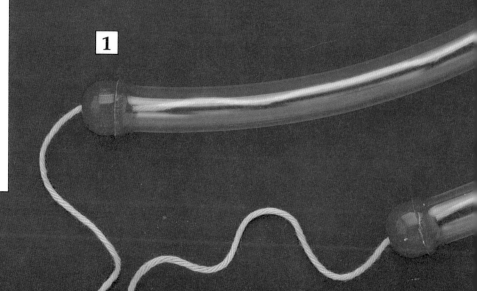

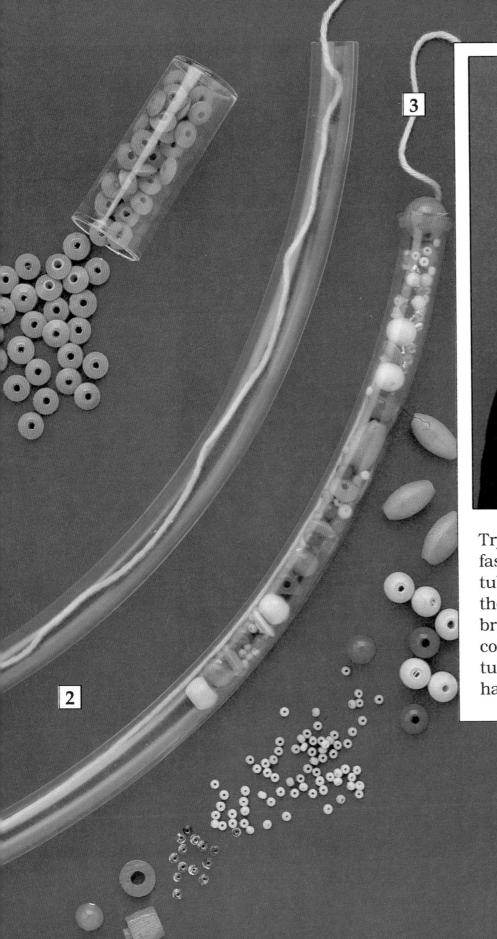

2

3

Try making a different necklace by fastening together several lengths of tube. You can leave the tubes clear, fill them with beads, or cover them with brightly colored tape. Try wrapping colored wool or glitter thread around a tube. Decorate your necklace with hanging beads and paper shapes.

15

Brooches

The first brooches were probably fastenings that kept the edges of a cloak or robe together. In Ireland over 1,400 years ago, noblemen and women wore brooches decorated with gold wire twisted and knotted into delicate lace patterns, and studded with semiprecious stones.

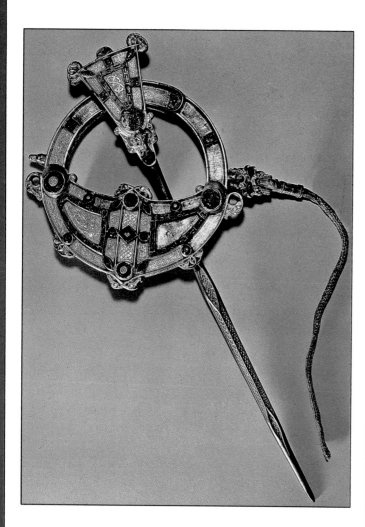

Look at pictures of jewelry from different countries to find some ideas for making your own.

Try designing and making a brooch

You will need:
- a pencil
- cardboard
- scrap paper
- scissors
- masking tape
- a bar pin or a safety pin
- latex-based glue
- strong transparent tape
- decorations such as beads, sequins, pipe cleaners, foil, shells, buttons, and gold paint

1 Cut a circle or other shape from cardboard to make a flat base for your brooch.

2 Crumple some scrap paper to cover the cardboard base. Squash the edges of the paper, but leave the center raised. Fasten it to the base with masking tape.

3 Stick several more strips of tape over the base to make a smooth surface.

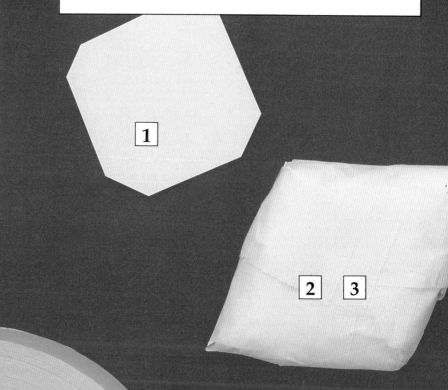

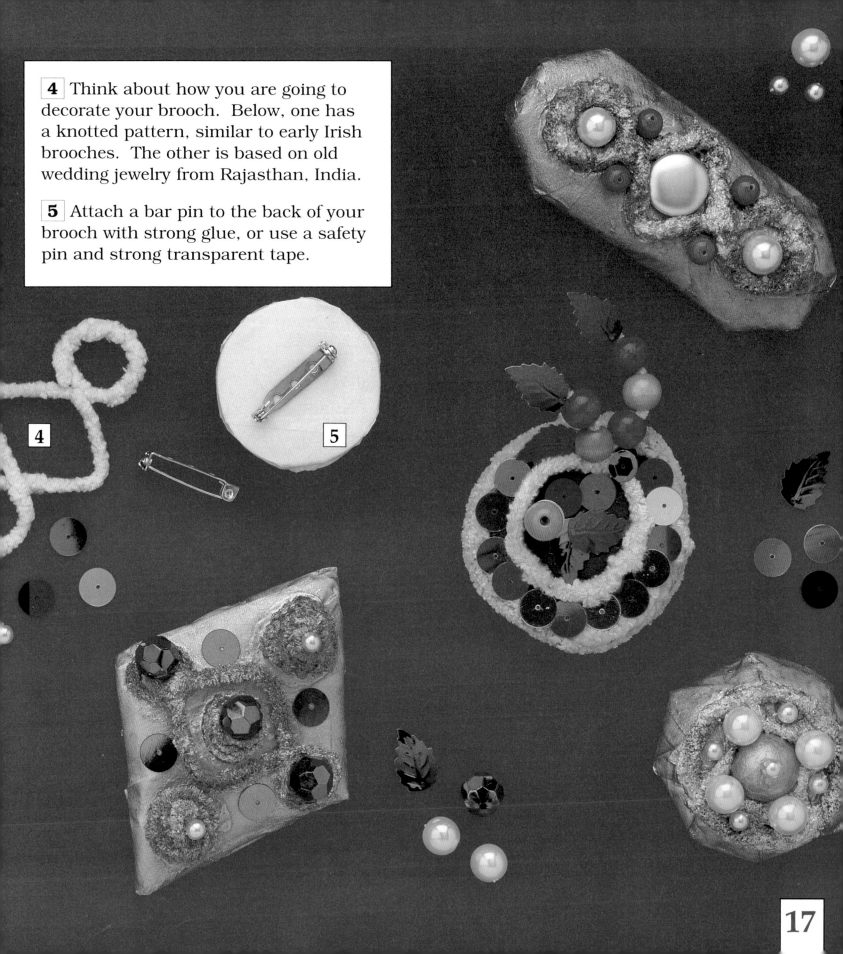

4 Think about how you are going to decorate your brooch. Below, one has a knotted pattern, similar to early Irish brooches. The other is based on old wedding jewelry from Rajasthan, India.

5 Attach a bar pin to the back of your brooch with strong glue, or use a safety pin and strong transparent tape.

4

5

Body language

Do you choose your clothes to suit your mood? Maybe sometimes you dress smartly to feel good about yourself; other times, you may dress to shock people. Do you wear different colors according to your mood?

A T-shirt showing words or symbols can tell people what your interests are. It may show the symbol of your favorite football team, a cartoon character you particularly like, or words describing something you care about, such as saving the rain forest.

In Ghana, there is a type of cloth called adinkra that used to be worn by royalty. It is hand printed with symbols, and each symbol has a special meaning. The colors also have meanings: white, for example, means joy or purity, while red means death or war. Adinkra cloth is very expensive to produce and is now only worn on very special occasions.

Try inventing your own signs and symbols. If one of your designs is very simple, you can make a printing block of it from a cardboard tube.

You will need:
- scrap paper
- cardboard tubes
- masking tape
- fabric paint
- poster paint
- a paintbrush
- a small plastic tray
- a plain cotton T-shirt
- a sheet of absorbent paper
- a strip of cardboard
- a plastic bag, roughly the same size as your T-shirt

Ask an adult if you can print your design on a plain T-shirt. You will need to use fabric paint to make your design permanent. Before you begin this activity, carefully read the instructions on the fabric paint.

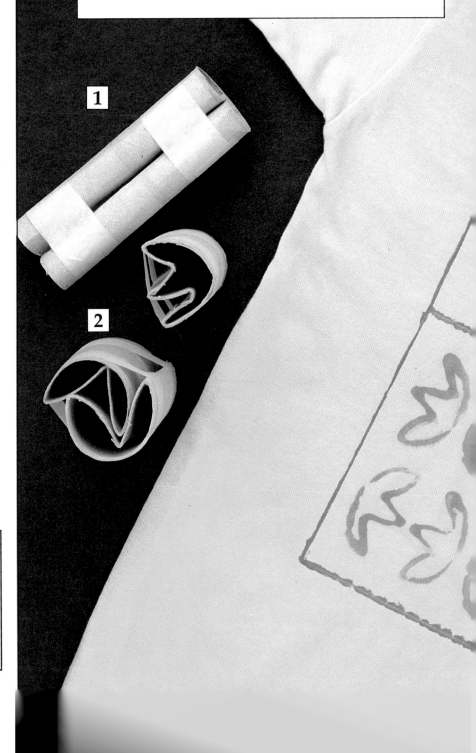

1 Experiment with squashing in the sides of some cardboard tubes to make shapes at the ends. Use masking tape to keep the tubes in shape.

2 You can tape the tubes together to make a more complicated pattern.

Pour a little poster paint into the tray. Dip one end of your tube shape into the paint and try printing different designs on paper.

3 Spread your T-shirt out flat. Place the plastic bag inside the shirt to stop the paint from going through to the back. Place the absorbent paper on top of the plastic to soak up any extra paint.

With the brush, put some fabric paint on the long edge of the cardboard strip and print four lines to make a large square on the T-shirt.

Carefully fill in the square with your printing block. Don't move the T-shirt until it is dry.

Instead of making one large square, you might make several smaller ones, using different printing blocks or colors.

You can also print your design on the back and sleeves of the T-shirt.

3

Tie-dye

Tie-dye is a process of decorating cloth that is popular all over the world. The patterns on tie-dyed cloth are made by tying thread around plain cloth. When the cloth is dyed, the parts of the cloth that have been tied do not absorb any of the color of the dye.

In Gambia, complicated patterns are made by tying and folding cloth in different ways. Sometimes a number of colored dyes are used. The woman in this picture is unfolding dyed cloth.

Try making a tie-dyed T-shirt with a spider's web pattern

You will need:
- a light-colored, plain T-shirt
- a packet of fabric dye
- an old bucket
- a sink with running water
- string
- pipe cleaners
- rubber bands
- scissors

Ask an adult to help you with this activity. It's best to use a dye that does not need a fixative. Before you begin, carefully read the instructions on the packet of dye.

1 Find the middle of the front of the T-shirt and pull it out to a point. Tie string, pipe cleaners, and rubber bands along the material to make a cone shape, as shown.

2 Tie a piece of string to the top of the cone shape and wrap it around the material to make a spiral. Knot it at the other end.

3 Mix the dye in the bucket, following the instructions carefully. Put your T-shirt in the dye and let it soak for as long as the instructions say.

It's best to remove the T-shirt from the dye over a sink. This will prevent the dye from staining any other surfaces. Rinse the T-shirt under a cold tap. Remove the string, rubber bands, and pipe cleaners.

Does the pattern on your T-shirt look like you thought it would?

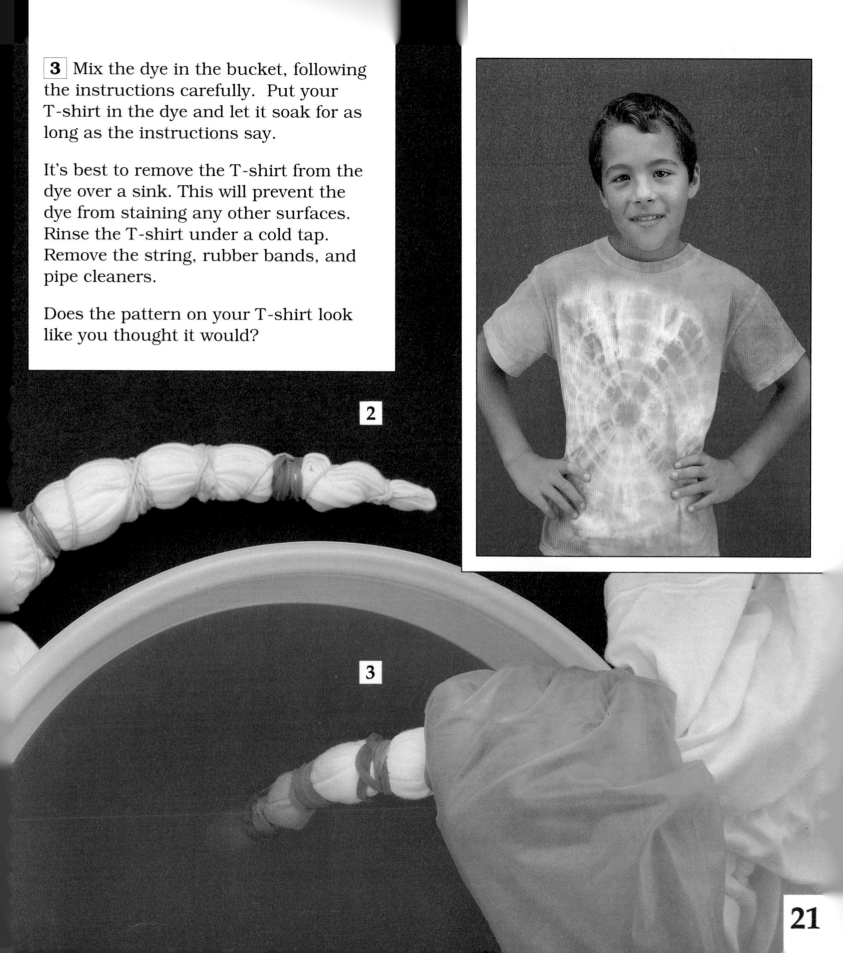

2

3

Decorated hands

Hands can be decorated with jewelry that has a special meaning. A wedding ring shows that someone is married, and a baby is often given a bracelet as a christening present. A kara, which is a steel bracelet, is worn by Sikhs as one of their special symbols. It represents the oneness of God and the kinship of the Sikhs.

Hands themselves can also be decorated. In India, there is a special form of hand decoration called mehndi, which can also be used to decorate feet. Designs are painted onto the hands and feet with fine lines, dots, and blocks of henna color. The patterns can be very intricate.

Make handprints on paper or draw around your hand, then draw your designs on the hand shapes.

Try decorating prints of your hands with symbols and patterns that say something about yourself. You can make signs that show your hobby, pet, or even your favorite food.

If you would like to try real mehndi, ask an adult's permission first. The design will stay on your hands for several days. Don't paint your hands if you have a rash or a skin allergy.

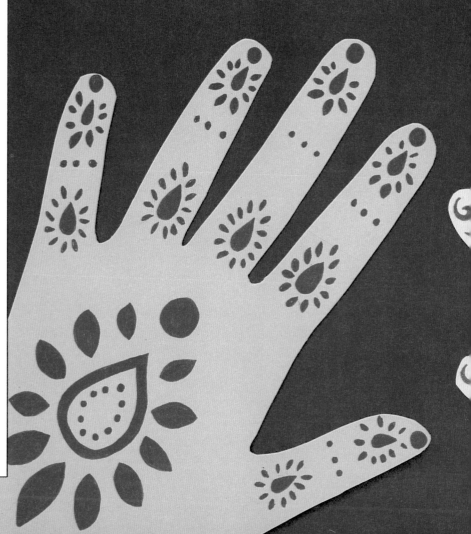

Dancing hands

Have you ever noticed how much some people use their hands when they are talking? Sometimes it helps them express themselves more clearly. Hands can also carry direct messages, such as when people wave good-bye or put their palms together in a greeting to say hello.

In classical ballet and many other dance styles, hand movements are used to help tell a story. Hand movements are very important in Indian Kathak dance. Kathak means "storyteller." Often, stories about Lord Krishna are told in dance.

This photograph shows a Kathak dancer moving her fingers as she dances.

As part of a special custom, the Inuit women of the Arctic sometimes wear finger puppets on their hands during dances.

Make an Inuit finger puppet

You will need:
- colored paper
- white glue or double-sided tape
- scissors
- a ruler

1 Cut out the paper shapes as shown: a circle a little larger than a large coin for the head; a strip 3/8 in. x 2 in. (1 cm x 5 cm) for the head-tab; two strips 4-3/4 in. x 3/4 in. (12 cm x 2 cm) for the body and the arms; a strip about 3/4 in. x 7 in. (2 cm x 18 cm) for the finger tubes.

2 To make the body, fold one strip in half to form a *V*-shape. Then fold back two tabs that are about 3/4 in. (2 cm). Glue the strip of paper together, except for the tabs at the end.

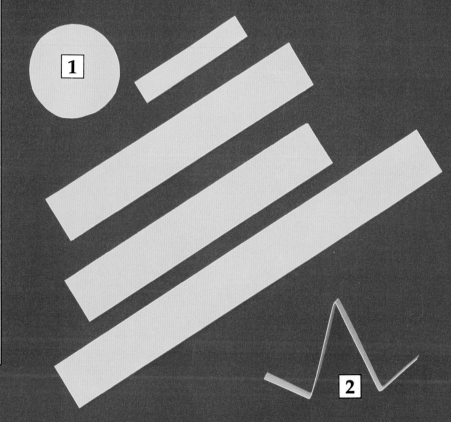

3 To make the arms, fold another strip in half. Fold out the arms 3/4 in. (2 cm) from the middle crease. Cut fingers and hands at each end of the arm.

4 To join the arms to the body, fold the middle crease of the arms around the base of the front of the body. The tops of the arms rest on the tabs, and the ends of the arms and hands are free. Glue in place.

5 Make finger tubes for your first and second fingers by rolling the paper in from each side and gluing in the middle.

6 To join the body to the finger tubes, glue the body-tabs to the finger tubes.

7 Fold the head-tab as shown.

8 Glue the middle of the head-tab to the back of the head, behind the chin.

9 To join the head to the body, glue the sides of the head-tabs around the sides of the front of the body. Decorate the head with paper shapes.

Wear your finger puppet on your first two fingers. Wriggle your fingers to make the puppet move.

Morris bells

Dancers often move to the rhythm of music played by musicians, but sometimes the dancers make some of the sounds themselves. German and Austrian folk dancing include movements where the dancers slap their thighs and shoes and stamp their feet to make a loud rhythmic noise.

Indian Kathak dancers and English morris dancers wear anklets of little tinkling bells, although the styles of dance are very different. Morris dancing is very energetic with lots of stamping, which makes the bells jingle furiously. The dancers usually move to the music of a fiddle or an accordion.

Try making a morris dance bell anklet

You will need:
- two pieces of felt, big enough to wrap around your ankle
- at least five little bells
- 1 yard (1 m) of ribbon
- a needle and thread
- glue
- scissors
- sequins and colored thread or wool for decoration

1 Cut one rectangular piece of felt so it nearly goes around your ankle. Cut another piece the same size. Thread the needle. Make a knot in one end of the thread. Sew the bells to one piece of felt securely, with several stitches for each bell. You can sew or glue sequins on for decoration if you wish. You can also embroider a simple pattern on the felt.

2 Cut the ribbon or tape into four pieces and sew or glue the pieces to the back of the felt with bells on it. To make the anklet stronger, sew or glue the second piece of felt to the back of the first.

Now tie the anklet around your ankle with the ribbons at the back. You are ready to dance!

Try making another anklet for your other leg.

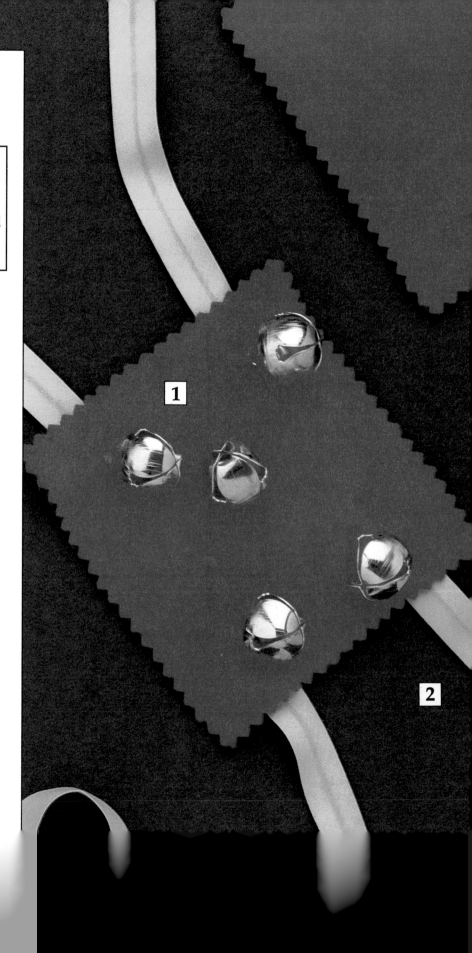

Wild feet

You may think that shoes just protect our soles on rough ground and keep our feet warm, but they can be much more than that. For example, Mercury, the Roman messenger of the gods, had wings on his sandals, and Cinderella had magic glass slippers. In Holland, St. Nicholas is said to leave Christmas presents in children's wooden clogs.

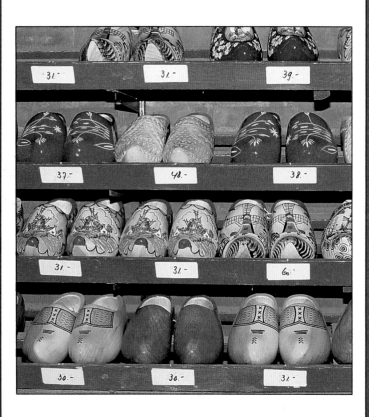

For many people, shoes are a vital part of their traditional dress; for others, they are an important fashion item.

Try transforming a pair of old canvas shoes

You will need:
- sequins
- felt
- scraps of fabric
- fabric pens
- beads
- old canvas shoes
- waterproof felt-tip pens
- lengths of colored ribbon or cord
- rubber cement

1 Look at the shape of your shoes carefully. Perhaps the shape suggests the face of an animal or a car. Cut out felt shapes for features such as wings, a tail, fins, or a hat. Decorate the shapes with beads, sequins, or fabric pens. Stick the felt shapes to the shoe with rubber cement.

2 Replace the shoelaces with lengths of colored ribbon or cord. Make tassels from felt or scraps of fabric and glue them to the ends of the laces.

3 Cut out a face shape, or any other shape you want, in felt. At the top of the shape, make two holes that are the same distance apart as the eye holes for the laces. Undo the laces or lengths of cord and thread the felt shape onto the front of the shoe.

4 Decorate the rubber toe-caps and ridges around the sole with sequins or patterns drawn with felt-tip pens.

1

2

3

4

More things to think about

This book shows you how to make and model papier-mâché, cut and fold paper, and print and dye cloth. You can use these different craft techniques to make your own costume crafts.

To get ideas for making your own crafts, think about the different ways we dress and decorate our bodies. Sometimes we dress to keep warm or cool, or sometimes we dress to say that we belong to a certain group. Do you ever dress in traditional clothes for special festival days?

Visit your local art gallery or museum to see how artists have shown people's clothes and jewelry now and in the past. Which clothes and decorations have changed most over the years? Which have stayed roughly the same? Can you find any ideas for modern clothes and other body decorations from old costumes and jewelry?

Many artists, sculptors, and craftspeople use the body as inspiration for their work. Try making a costume craft project, concentrating on one part of the body, such as the hands, feet, or face. Think of all the ways that people from around the world have decorated this part of their body, now and long ago.

Look at the shape of your hands, feet, or face. Draw around them and then draw huge and tiny versions. Try making printing blocks using these shapes. How would you make an interesting pattern on paper or fabric from these repeated shapes? How could you make the shapes of your hands, feet, and face three-dimensional?

Before starting your project, think about the best craft technique to use. For example, you can make and model papier-mâché, cut and fold paper, or print and dye cloth. Do you want to wear the object? Will it help to keep you warm or cool? Is it just for decoration? Think carefully about the best way of making your craft project and the best materials to use.

Think about the various ways you can create different textures, colors, and shades with paper, cloth, or by modeling papier-mâché. Try recreating the texture of wool, lace, or precious stones. Think about patterns to decorate your project. Look for patterns in brickwork, trees, the coats of animals, or cross sections of fruit.

For more information

More books to read

Adventures in Art
   Susan Milford (Williamson)

Beads
   Judy Ann Sadler (Kids Can)

Dress Up
   Sarah Lynn and Diane James
   (Bantam Books)

Five Minute Faces
   Snazaroo (Random House)

Friendship Bracelets
   Camilla Gryski (Beech Tree)

Fun with Fabric
   Juliet Bawden (Random House)

Hats
   Claire Beaton (Franklin Watts)

Kids Create
   Laurie Carlson (Williamson)

The Kids Multicultural Art Book
   Alexandra Terzian (Williamson)

Living Long Ago: Clothes and Fashion
   Felicity Brooks (Usborne)

*Make Believe: A Book of Costume
   and Fantasy*
   (Klutz Press)

Make Clothes Fun
   Kim Solga (North Light)

60 Art Projects for Children
   Jeannette M. Baumgardner
   (Clarkson Potter)

Videos

Anessi's Barkcloth Art (Coronet)

Don't Eat the Pictures
   (Children's Television Workshop)

Look What I Made: Paper Playthings and Gifts

My First Activity Video (Sony)

Yohannes the Silversmith (Coronet)

Places to visit

The following places have major collections of crafts from around the world. Don't forget to look in your area museum, too.

Canadian Museum of Civilization
100 Laurier Street
P.O. Box 3100, Station B
Hull, Quebec
J8X 4H2

Denver Museum of Natural History
2001 Colorado Boulevard
Denver, Colorado 80205

Franklin Institute
20th Street and the Franklin Parkway
Philadelphia, Pennsylvania 19103-1194

Royal British Columbia Museum
675 Belleville Street
Victoria, British Columbia
V8V 1X4

The Smithsonian Institution
1000 Jefferson Drive SW
Washington, D.C. 20560

Index

For a free color catalog describing Gareth Stevens' list of high-quality books, call 1-800-542-2595 (USA) or 1-800-461-9120 (Canada). Gareth Stevens' Fax: (414) 225-0377.

Library of Congress
Cataloging-in-Publication Data
MacLeod-Brudenell, Iain.
    Costume crafts/Iain MacLeod-Brudenell; photographs by Zul Mukhida.
    North American ed.
    p. cm. — (Worldwide crafts)
    Includes bibliographical references and index.
    ISBN 0-8368-1152-6
    1. Handicraft—Juvenile literature. 2. Paper work—Juvenile literature. 3. Dress accessories—Juvenile literature. [1. Handicraft. 2. Paper work. 3. Dress accessories.] I. Mukhida, Zul, ill. II. Title. III. Series.
TT160.M2586 1994
745.5—dc20   94-11432

North American edition first published in 1994 by
Gareth Stevens Publishing
1555 North RiverCenter Drive, Suite 201
Milwaukee, Wisconsin 53212, USA

First published in 1993 by A & C Black (Publishers) Limited, London; © 1993 A & C Black (Publishers) Limited.

Acknowledgments
Line drawings by Barbara Pegg.
Photographs by Zul Mukhida, except for:
p. 8, p. 22, p. 24 Compix; p. 12 British Museum; p. 16 Bridgeman Art Library; p. 20, p. 28 Life File Photographic Agency; p. 26 Robert Harding Picture Library

Grateful thanks to Langford and Hill, Ltd., London, for supplying all art materials.

Crafts made by Dorothy Moir except for those on pp. 4-5, 14-15, 18-19, 26-27, which were made by Tracy Brunt.

Printed in the United States of America

1 2 3 4 5 6 7 8 9 9 99 98 97 96 95 94

At this time, Gareth Stevens, Inc., does not use 100 percent recycled paper, although the paper used in our books does contain about 30 percent recycled fiber. This decision was made after a careful study of current recycling procedures revealed their dubious environmental benefits. We will continue to explore recycling options.